ADHD Is Bullshit

Unmasking The Truth

Jessica Carrier, CTNC, HHP

Disclosure

The book's title: "ADHD is Bullshit," is meant to do what it did: Capture your attention. If you are a person who is easily offended by taboo language or you are closed-minded - this book may not be for you. If you like to hear from someone who is both educated and speaks casually but gives it to you straight up, then let's dive TF in! But before you do, you should know some things.

I am neither a medical doctor nor a Ph.D. I do not directly or indirectly diagnose disease, dispense medical advice, or prescribe products or services to treat sickness or disease. This information is for educational purposes only. You should always do your research and cooperate with the health professional of your choice with a mutual goal of building good health. This book is not medical advice. This information is from my private research, public studies, personal experience, and observation.
The Food and Drug Administration has not evaluated the statements made in this book. These statements represent the opinions of the author.
I do not claim to "cure" ADHD or any other condition. You should follow package instructions for food and supplements over what is listed here. Consult with a licensed medical professional before beginning any supplement regimen.
Do not do a heavy metal detox or elimination diet if you are pregnant or nursing,
Undergoing or recovering from surgery, have extreme nutrient deficiencies, severe weakness, Type 1 Diabetes, Experience Seizures, or are currently under a doctor's care for a disease or medical condition.
Do not discontinue the use of medications without first consulting with your trusted medical healthcare provider.
I prefer a holistic approach to health care; however, I am not "anti-medical." There very much is a place in my family for conventional medical care (allopathic medicine) that we rely on and are very grateful for!

While you will find in this book that I stress the importance of taking your health into your own hands, it is essential to note that If you or a family member have a mental illness, please seek help from a professional and do not attempt to self-diagnose. Should you disagree with the diagnosis of said professional, I encourage you to seek a second or sometimes third opinion. If you choose to avoid medications, I recommend natural wellness doctors and Functional Medicine Doctors to assist you in seeking answers!

One day, I hope this book will be irrelevant to the world because that will mean we changed it.

To my incredible boys, who inspire me every day to unmask the truth and embrace the extraordinary. You are my greatest teachers, and this book is a testament to our shared resilience & my love for you.

bull·shit

/ˈbool̩SHit/

Vulgar Slang

Noun: stupid or untrue talk or writing; nonsense.
Verb: talk nonsense to (someone), typically to be misleading or deceptive.

Contents

Preface

I'm sure you have heard of sensitive skin. Well, everyone loves a good metaphor, right?

Sensitive skin reacts adversely to things such as skincare products, soaps, and fabrics. People with sensitive skin often deal with discomfort, redness, irritation, itching, and sometimes even a burning sensation when they encounter certain substances that don't affect other people. Those people are cautious about products, and for good reason!

Similarly, type 2 diabetics, who are sensitive to insulin level fluctuations, carefully manage their sugar intake. Those with celiac disease, sensitive to gluten, steer clear of wheat, barley, and rye. Someone with a peanut allergy takes precautions by avoiding nuts.

Imagine if someone had dangerous blood sugar spikes, rashes on their skin, severe stomach issues, swelling in the throat, and dizziness. Instead of treating each condition individually, as mentioned above, the doctor labels this person as "broken" and gives them a pill that tricks the body into thinking nothing's wrong when internally it's breaking down. That would be absurd! Well, it's actually not so unheard of when it comes to treating the mind.

Because mental illness is not evident from a scan or blood test, "collections" of symptoms create the diagnosis. That's where Attention Deficit Hyperactivity Disorder (ADHD) comes into the picture—it's a catch-all term coined in the late 1980s and widely used to label individuals experiencing many unexplained mental symptoms ranging from hyperactivity and impulsiveness to disorganization and forgetfulness and so much more.

ADHD is now a multi-billion dollar industry. Healthcare providers prescribe medications like stimulants and non-stimulants to manage ADHD symptoms, generating substantial revenue for pharmaceutical corporations. Some argue that there's a financial incentive to maintain ADHD diagnoses and manage symptoms rather than pursuing potential alternatives or exploring the possibility of healing or coping without medication.

I invite you to consider that each ADHD symptom could have its own explanation and solution. ADHD is the brain's reaction to various stressors, just like sensitive skin. With the elimination of those stressors, the brain can thrive. Where's the science to prove it? Deep in the trenches because no one makes money off of health.
We'll explore what it can look like when the brain responds to inconsistent surroundings, toxic food, heavy metals, nutritional deficiencies, and much more, starting with my personal journey through hell.

1

Where The Bullshit Began

Looking back at my childhood, I was the poster child for an undiagnosed, non-medicated young girl with ADHD. Reading was a struggle, and I relied on friends to give me quick summaries of books before tests. I never got awards for accelerated reading, and I spent all of my recess time playing catch up which made school rather shitty for me.

Once I got a bad taste in my mouth for school, I struggled to turn things around. Inability to focus, impulsiveness, lousy decision-making, and horrible grades were part of my everyday life. However, since I was incredibly creative, could hyper-focus on solutions at the last minute, and always found a way to cover up my mistakes, nobody acknowledged my challenges, and I could fly under the radar. Without the help I needed, I spent several years feeling broken and downright stupid. Instead of asking for help, I would put on a mask. As an attempted distraction, I would cause chaos among friends and rebel against teachers. I remember plotting, "I would rather them think I'm an asshole than to think I'm stupid" Somehow, even with poor attendance, I managed to graduate high school, serve in the military, and complete my journeyman in Information Technology without anyone calling me out. Still, despite these accomplishments, I couldn't shake the feeling that my intelligence was inferior and that I was "less of a person than those around me."

It wasn't only my mental well-being that suffered; my physical health was always in disarray. I oscillated between excessive sleep and insomnia, constantly battled tummy aches, and perpetually felt exhausted. As a baby, I had colic; as a child, I suffered from eczema; and as a teen, illness seemed to be the norm.

Unfortunately, there was never a time for self-exploration in my young adult years, as I found out I was pregnant with twins at 20.

Two babies on the way meant I had to suppress my struggles and be a good mom, or so I thought.

Little did I know, they would not only change my life but also be the answer to all the lingering doubts I had about myself.

Pardon me as I get a little cheesy, but they were the absolute sweetest babies, and the toddler years were enjoyable! Their personalities constantly kept me laughing.

It didn't take long to learn that, unfortunately. The poor things inherited their momma's neuro-symptoms.

Unlike me, they couldn't mask themselves as daydreamers because they were locked and loaded with hyperactivity, opposition, and sensory issues! Skipping the crawling stages, they took off walking right away! The fabric in their clothing had to be just right, and the lighting in the house was dim to keep them calm. These flukes were manageable until around the age of seven. Bedtime had become a battleground- they refused to sleep, visiting stores and attending events always turned into chaos due to being overstimulated by too many people and bright lights, and constant fighting between them became the soundtrack of our lives. They seemed to have an aversion to following directions!

The pressure from both sides of the family, friends, and society on how children should behave was suffocating. People either criticized me for being too hard on them or whispered behind my back that I wasn't hard enough. Gatherings with both family and friends became nightmares of constant judgment. Desperate for peace and social life, I even resorted to bribery with candy and gifts so they would "act good" around certain people. I thought I had tried everything, but as the saying goes, "You don't know what you don't know." Their hyperactivity, my internal chaos, my husband's frustrations, and relentless judgment from everyone created a living hell for all of us. Even in the depths of the fire, I and a select few could see - they were still unique little humans with hearts of gold whose little brains were struggling.

The fire got too hot.

I eventually hit rock bottom and found myself screaming like a psycho in response to their behavior. It was as if one day, they woke up and didn't give a shit what I had to say. They pushed back hard, and I was at my wit's end! I soon sought help from a doctor who referred us to a child psychiatrist. The diagnostic process was shockingly straightforward. We filled out forms ahead of time, both parents and a teacher, and then had a brief 15-20 minute session with the doctor. That was it. She casually diagnosed them with ADHD, prescribed medication with no cure in sight, and recommended therapy for the defiant symptoms. There were no medical tests or investigations to rule out other possibilities. It was a quick and straightforward verdict: ADHD. I walked out of that clinic in a daze, oblivious to all the red flags waving around me.

Against every fiber of my being as a mother, I reluctantly gave my boys their first pill. Within 30 minutes, it was as if someone hit the mute button, and everything fell into serene stillness. Like stepping out of a crowded amusement park into the peacefulness of a quiet meadow, the commotion had ceased, allowing me to catch my breath and find a moment of tranquility. My children seemed genuinely happy and calm. The next day, their teachers praised their newfound "good behavior." It felt like I had found the golden solution to their struggles.

I learned in family therapy that their defiance potentially stemmed from inconsistent parenting and confusion arising from multiple different styles of authority figures in their life. This made so much sense: A free-spirited mom paired with a more conventional father at home (undermining each other left and right), a kind and compassionate teacher one year, followed up the next year with someone completely unhinged. Pair that with family members who would purposely break my rules and openly criticize me in front of them. A confusing environment paired with underlying brain health conditions did not allow these two young children to grasp what was right and wrong. During this time, I took it upon myself to do some inner work. I couldn't change the a-holes around me, but I could work on myself. I revisited the fact that I, too, had ADHD symptoms, and that largely contributed to being an inconsistent parent. I created a plan to establish consistency with my parenting style, weed out all the noise from others, and distance my kiddos from toxic friends and family members. As I implemented this positive change, the opposition ceased to exist.

Life was genuinely great until, out of nowhere, the impulsiveness, memory issues, and inability to focus quickly resurfaced, eroding the progress made by the medication & therapy. The chaos returned, and with it, my inconsistencies as a parent. This led back to defiance - pushing us back down to the bottom.

Back at the complete mercy of the doctor, I booked another appointment for an ADHD checkup. The doctor who had diagnosed the boys and started them on medication was no longer working there. The new doctor, just as casual as the first, increased the prescription dosage. This dance continued for some time, and trips to the doctor became a never-ending journey that wore down my boys to the point where they would cry at the mere mention of having an appointment. Despite the hardships, I persisted, hoping to regain those moments of tranquility when they were happy, functioning, and calm.

Then, one year into this medication madness, I received a call from the school that sent my world into a tailspin. An emergency was occurring with one of the boys. I rushed to the school, beating the ambulance, only to find my child lying on the cafeteria floor, clutching his chest, struggling to breathe, and suffering from a dangerously high heart rate. Panicked, I rushed him to the hospital, where the doctor said to discontinue the ADHD medication immediately. I'm unsure if I heard anything after this as my mind got stuck on repeat, wondering how or why the doctor could so quickly conclude that the medication was the culprit. Then it hit me like a ton of bricks! Was I so desperate to give my children pills without thoroughly reading the side effects? Better yet, had I just spent the past year having doctors treat them for a condition without even educating myself? Sadly, yes. Out of desperation, I surrendered to big pharma and trusted the medical establishment with the care of my child. A week later, I visited a cardiologist at Children's Hospital with my son, where we learned that he had, in fact, experienced an adverse reaction to ADHD medications combined with a major anxiety attack! At this time, I felt defeated, again exhausted, and the home I had built was in shambles.

Filled with remorse, I embarked on an intensive research journey to understand ADHD and the medications used to treat it. I also researched how the public school system's structure, lighting, and chaos worsened ADHD symptoms.

In addition, I learned that ADHD medications double as street drugs. WHAT?!? How did I miss all of this? How could I have exposed my children to such substances? The same pill I gave my kid to manage his chaotic brain was the same shit people were using to get jacked up on the weekends? This information made me wonder, "Did the medication make them high? Was that what the stillness was? Is this all my fault? Is it genetic?" These questions, coupled with the weight of mom guilt, my intense love for my family, and my compassion for my inner child, ignited a deep desire for change. I knew medication therapy, specifically controlled substances, was out of the picture, and I recognized the need for further personal growth and healing. I was determined to ensure that the chaos that had ruled my childhood and my children's rough start would not define any of us. I set out on a mission to find better answers.

On this journey, I discovered that my childhood mental and physical symptoms were far from ordinary, and I also realized that I was never "stupid." Multiple IQ tests proved that neither I nor my children were intellectually inferior to our peers; quite the opposite. After embarking on this healing journey, I accomplished remarkable feats that I couldn't have imagined as a child, such as reading an entire series of books in under three weeks (where's my accelerated reader award now?) and successfully applying newly acquired skills in multiple businesses that I built from the ground up. I learned that I could focus perfectly on my interests and learn QUICKLY. So could my kids.

Is it starting to sound like I'm leading up to a fairy tale ending? Sorry, I'm FAR FROM IT! Listen, I live in a small town in the Midwest. Anyone trying anything new creates a lot of talk. This journey has been lonely. I have lost friends, been met with extreme judgment, overheard whispers behind my back by family, and experienced disgusting betrayal. This experience was all because I hyper-focused my entire existence, researching, experimenting, testing, and finding solutions for my children.

The brokenness that stemmed from all of this is still mending. Still, I would do it all over again, experiencing every bit of hurt and frustration if I knew I could help my babies or anyone else from experiencing the pain of living with a condition that provides minimal answers. The holistic solutions I found were not only UNBELIEVABLE and life-changing for us, but they have made a difference in the lives of many others. So, what did I ultimately learn? Well, here's a little hint: read the title.

In the preceding chapters, I will challenge the medical establishments' status quo and take you on an exploration of neuroscience to unravel ADHD. I will help you discover what could be causing your symptoms and teach you to embrace the remarkable aspects of not quite fitting in. Along the way, I will share more of our personal experiences in healing and more on how our lives have dramatically changed.

2

Chasing Zebras

Have you ever seen those videos where a tiny person full of adrenaline lifts a car off someone?

A momma on a mission is a similar phenomenon. I didn't just dabble in research; I didn't just settle for generic advice. I sank my heels in and went ALL OUT!

I TESTED EVERYTHING!

I soon learned that my and my kid's ADHD symptoms stemmed from food product sensitivities, chaotic environments, nutrient deficiencies, hormonal imbalances, retained primitive reflexes, gut disturbances, lack of beneficial gut bacteria, heavy metal toxicity, and genetic mutations!

It sounds wild, I know. You may think: "If there are so many possible explanations for what could be causing my ADHD symptoms, why didn't my doctor dig further?" The short answer lies in the allopathic medical lingo that makes me cringe: "Chasing Zebras." This term is used in medicine, even taught in medical school, to describe a situation where if a common diagnosis looks good on paper, there's no need to look further into it. The saying is actually, "When you hear hoofbeats, don't look for zebras." Meaning that the likely cause of the sound of hoofbeats is a horse. Unfortunately, this happens all too often - a quick diagnosis of something familiar without considering what makes up the whole, very unique, person.

When this happens, and you aren't comfortable with the answers, it may be a sign to take control of your or your child's health like I did.

I thought I was alone on this journey until I learned the difference between functional and allopathic medicine.

Allopathic medicine treats specific symptoms or diseases with drugs, surgeries, and other interventions. It often relies on evidence-based practices and aims to alleviate symptoms or cure diseases.

Functional medicine, on the other hand, takes a more holistic approach. It seeks to address the **root causes** of illnesses and promote overall wellness by considering various factors like genetics, lifestyle, environment, and diet.
Many of us wouldn't be alive today if it weren't for the life-saving techniques and medications rooted in allopathic medicine; however, conventional treatment plans for ADHD rely mainly on dangerous drugs that can mask what's really going on at the root of it all.

Controlled substances come with a range of dangerous side effects that should be considered, such as hypertension, rapid heartbeat, insomnia (which often requires additional sleep medication to counteract), appetite suppression (leading to binge eating once the effects of the drug wear off), overdose, sudden cardiac death, stroke, headache, constipation, mood swings, abdominal pain, depression, panic attacks, psychosis, kidney disease, seizures, muscle weakness, bladder weakness, and sexual dysfunction.

I'm not trying to gather a group of self-diagnosed hypochondriacs who rely on Dr. Google. I'm advocating for the pursuit of our own answers and seeking alternatives that conventional medical systems may not have the time to provide. When you hear hoofbeats but believe in your gut that it's not a horse, you may have to find your zebras!

In the upcoming chapters, I'll take you through everything I uncovered with myself and my children on our zebra-chasing journey.

Do not discontinue medication without the support and supervision of a trusted medical provider. Abruptly stopping medications can often lead to worsening symptoms and, in tragic cases, even death.

3

DevelopMENTAL Hurdles

My initial discovery led us to a kick-ass natural wellness doc who blew our minds with some real eye-opening stuff about retained primitive reflexes!

Survival Instinct

From tiny infants to curious toddlers, our bodies take us through a wild ride of development. We are born with automatic moves wired into our nervous system. We call these early moves "primitive reflexes," they're here to lend us a hand when we're just starting. For example, the Moro Reflex, also known as a baby's "startle reflex," occurs when a baby is lying on their back and experiences a sudden loud noise, a quick movement, or even a sensation of falling. The baby reacts by spreading their arms, fingers splayed apart, and slightly arching their back. They eventually bring their arms back together toward their body, sometimes even clutching their fists. This reflex is an instinctual response designed to protect the baby from potential danger. As we grow, reflexes such as this one are supposed to step aside and make room for purposeful, intentional actions that we can control.

Now, in some folks, these primitive reflexes don't get the memo to take a hike. That's what we call "retained primitive reflexes." While these lingering reflexes might not immediately mess things up, they can set the stage for many challenges, including brain hiccups that can look like ADHD. Reasons for retained reflexes range from genetic factors to nervous system imbalance and skipped milestones like crawling.

ADHD Symptom Overlap

Retained primitive reflexes can appear in many ways, causing everything from motor issues to sensory sensitivities. For example, the startle reflex I mentioned, if kept, might make you all impulsive, restless, and forgetful! Individuals with this reflex can also be easily overwhelmed and have a heightened sensitivity to stress.

When reflexes like the Asymmetrical Tonic Neck Reflex (ATNR) overstay their welcome, fine motor skills, focus, and coordination difficulties can appear. The symmetrical Tonic Neck Reflex (STNR), on the other hand, when retained, can lead to issues sitting still, fidgeting, and maintaining posture.

ALL CLASSIC ADHD VIBES!

Help With Primitive Reflexes

With the help of our natural wellness doctor, we discovered the boys had nearly half a dozen retained primitive reflexes running the show.

After committing to a six-month regimen of nightly exercises, we started to see some positive changes – less hyperactivity and improved speech, to be precise.

While there's debate about whether primitive reflexes can cause ADHD-like symptoms, I can vouch that integrating them can make a real difference. Many specialists offer free initial consultations if you want to explore this further. Look for "Primitive Reflex Integration Therapy" – a service available through various professionals, including physical therapists, some chiropractors, developmental pediatricians, and neurologists.

Later, we dive into vitamin deficiencies, heavy metals, gene mutations, and food-induced ADHD. But before that, we're going to talk about the gut. In obtaining my holistic health certificate, I learned that the digestive system is number one on the health ladder, and for a darn good reason: if the gut isn't up to snuff, then whatever you do with medications, vitamins, and nutrition might as well take a trip to the land of lost causes.

4

Do You Have The Guts?

While the gut's reputation often revolves around digestion, it's a powerhouse extending its influence beyond food processing. From amping up your body's natural defenses to shaping your emotions and thoughts, the gut quietly ensures that your physical and mental states are in perfect harmony.

Genius Factory

Did you know the gut is intelligent? The network of neurons orchestrating digestion is called the Enteric Nervous System. This system is not just a processing plant for the food you eat. Some scientists call it the second brain. Recent studies show that this system can work independently from your central brain, influencing emotions and reactions.

If you've ever trusted your intuition by "following your gut" to make a choice or experienced those "butterflies in your stomach" during moments of nervousness, you're probably tuning into your body's second brain.

For many years, researchers and doctors held the notion that mental health conditions played a part in the development of gut issues; however, discoveries suggest it may be the opposite. It seems that the interaction between mental health, mood, and cognitive functioning could be multidirectional.

Communication Department

Here's the deal: An entire community of microorganisms resides primarily in your large intestine. These microorganisms include bacteria, viruses, fungi, and other single-celled organisms. Now, "What's their gig," you ask? They're on a mission to keep all things in balance. They help you digest food, absorb nutrients, and even protect you from harmful invaders.

On top of that, they're also releasing neurotransmitters directly to the brain. Picture it as if they're firing off text messages with mood-altering emojis, stress-busting gifs, and thought-provoking memes. And guess what? Your brain's reading every note loud and clear.

That's not where it ends, though. Your brain doesn't just read those messages; it talks back! It's a rhythmic production that keeps your entire body in perfect harmony - like your body's communication department. So, if you ever wondered why a tummy ache can make you feel off mentally or why stress can mess with your digestion, you're witnessing this back-and-forth exchange in action.

Broken Equipment

So, what happens when communication errors occur? Digestive conditions like leaky gut, malabsorption, IBS, dysbiosis, and celiac disease can cause damage to the gut, which in turn sends mixed signals and potentially toxic substances directly to the brain.

The biggest hurdle is that many of these conditions are not always evident. A condition like a leaky gut can go undiagnosed forever because its symptoms can be unrelated to the gut!

The medical term for "leaky gut" is "increased intestinal permeability." It refers to a condition in which the lining of the small intestine becomes more permeable, allowing substances that should be contained within the digestive tract to pass through and enter the bloodstream.

When you have a leaky gut, toxic substances can enter the bloodstream. Some will pass the blood-brain barrier, overloading your brain with toxins and causing inflammation. Inflammation can manifest as allergies, weight fluctuations, nutritional deficiencies, cognitive disruption, and, you guessed it, classic ADHD symptoms like inattention, hyperactivity, and emotional dysregulation!

Short Staffed

For some individuals, microbiota diversity is scarce or "short-staffed." This lack of workers affects neurotransmitter production, leading to difficulties in concentration, fluctuations in mood balance, memory lapses, and reduced cognitive clarity.

Early life circumstances that can cause a lack of diversity in the microbiome are c-section delivery, early use of Tylenol, gastrointestinal infections, overuse of antibiotics, and not being breastfed.

Field Test

A variety of tests are available that can answer any concerns you may have about your gut health and let you know if your gut is contributing to your ADHD symptoms. These tests include Intestinal Permeability Tests, GI Map Tests, Zonulin Testing, and Comprehensive stool analysis. My favorite is the Organic Acid Test.

Organic Acid Test (OAT): This test can provide information about metabolites produced by gut bacteria, which can indirectly indicate the health of your gut microbiome. The OAT test also shows vitamin deficiencies. It provides insights into how your body is processing nutrients and energy. It can provide information about potential gut dysbiosis and the presence of harmful microorganisms. My favorite part: The OAT test offers insights into brain health, the balance of neurotransmitters associated with mood and cognitive function, and much more.

My kid's results on this test were astounding. We found vitamin deficiencies and insights about their inability to produce glutathione, essential to digestion and detoxification. We also discovered a lack of diversity in the microbiome and much more!

Back In Business

Now that we've uncovered the remarkable role of the gut in our overall well-being and we have discussed available testing, it's time to roll up our sleeves and start the journey toward getting our damn minds right. The gut is a complex ecosystem, and just like a successful production factory, it requires proper care, maintenance, and staff to thrive.

Take a break from certain foods and incorporate gut-friendly food. Some foods are tough on the gut, especially in the case of a leaky gut. If you suspect you have a leaky gut, taking a break from the following foods may give your gut a chance to heal: processed food, gluten, dairy, sugars, alcohol, and caffeine. Instead, spend your energy incorporating healing nutrients from foods such as

Fiber-rich Foods: Non-starchy vegetables, fruits, whole grains, and legumes can provide prebiotic fibers supporting healthy gut microbiota.

Fermented Foods: Yogurt, kefir, sauerkraut, kimchi, and kombucha are examples of fermented foods that can introduce beneficial probiotics to your gut. Be careful that your yogurt isn't loaded with sugar; otherwise, it defeats the purpose.

Healthy Fats: Include healthy fats like avocados, olive oil, nuts, and seeds, which can help reduce inflammation and support gut health. **Great for brain health, too!

Bone Broth: Some people find bone broth, rich in collagen and amino acids, can help soothe and repair the gut lining.

Lean Proteins: Opt for lean protein sources such as poultry, fish, and plant-based proteins.

Dietary changes alone may not fully address leaky gut, and it's important to address underlying causes and consider additional lifestyle factors like

Mindful Eating: Your healing journey begins right at your plate. Adopting mindful eating practices can significantly impact your gut health. Slow down and savor each bite, paying attention to the flavors, textures, and sensations. Chew your food thoroughly, as digestion begins in the mouth. Chewing allows your gut to work more efficiently and extract vital food nutrients.

Stay Hydrated: Drinking enough water supports proper digestion and helps maintain the mucosal lining of your gut. Opt for filtered water to minimize exposure to contaminants that might disrupt gut health.

Probiotics and Prebiotics: Probiotics are the friendly bacteria that promote gut health, while prebiotics are the fibers that feed these bacteria.

Include probiotic-rich foods like yogurt, kefir, sauerkraut, and kimchi. Prebiotic sources include garlic, onions, bananas, and asparagus.

Reduce Stress: Chronic stress can wreak havoc on your gut—practice stress-reduction techniques like meditation, deep breathing, yoga, and time in nature. A calm mind contributes to a calm gut.

Quality Sleep: Prioritize quality sleep to allow your body and gut to repair and regenerate. Aim for 7-9 hours of uninterrupted sleep each night.

Exercise Regularly: Physical activity supports gut motility and overall health. Find an exercise routine that you enjoy and can stick to.

Manage Medications: Some medications can impact gut health. Work with your healthcare provider to explore alternative medicines or strategies that minimize their effects on the gut.

Minimize Antibiotics: While antibiotics are essential in certain situations, overuse can disrupt the balance of your gut microbiota. Only take antibiotics when necessary and prescribed by a healthcare professional. Even then, you can discuss your concerns about the overuse of antibiotics, discuss alternative options, and consider probiotic supplementation during and after antibiotic treatment.

Limit Toxin Exposure: Reduce exposure to environmental toxins and harmful chemicals that can disrupt gut health. Choose organic produce, avoid plastic containers, and use natural cleaning and personal care products.

Consider Supplementation: In some cases, targeted supplementation may be beneficial. Consult a healthcare provider to determine if you need specific supplements such as probiotics, digestive enzymes, or nutrients that support gut health.

Healing your gut is a personal journey, and what does the trick for one might not cut it for another.

Tune in to your body, feel how it reacts to different changes in your diet and lifestyle, and remember to go easy on yourself. It's the little, steady steps that can create some seriously impressive improvements in your gut health and cognitive functioning.

Now that we know about the intelligent exchange between our gut and brain let's explore the line of communication—the vagus nerve. This neural highway is the path that connects the depths of our gut to the far reaches of our brain!

5

The Nerve

Another Path From The Gut To The Brain
The Vagus Nerve

Remember the gut-brain connection we dug into earlier? We saw how the gut and the brain are like BFFs, sending messages back and forth and what can happen when those conversations hit a snag. Well, think of the vagus nerve as one of the hotlines handling this exchange of info plus more. More than a conduit, it's also the queen B in charge of keeping stress, inflammation, and sensory stuff in check. Unfortunately, the vagus nerve can run into problems thanks to chronic inflammation, unresolved trauma, or underlying health issues.

Should these disruptions occur, bodily functions, including digestion, heart rate, and even mood regulation, get all jacked up. In addition, a range of symptoms that mimic ADHD, such as inattentiveness, sensory issues, mood swings, and impulsivity, might manifest.

Vagus Nerve Self-Assessment

Understanding whether vagus nerve disruption might be contributing to your ADHD symptoms or other health problems involves observing your body's responses and patterns. Keep in mind that while these signs could point to vagus nerve issues, they may also indicate other health concerns.

- **Digestive Distress:** If you frequently experience indigestion, bloating, constipation, or a feeling of fullness after eating, it might be a digestive issue, but it could also be a sign of vagus nerve imbalance affecting digestion.
- **Heart Rate Variability:** An irregular heart rate or sudden heart rate changes, especially during rest or relaxation, could indicate vagus nerve issues. Also, if your heart rate doesn't return to its baseline after strenuous activity relatively quickly, it might reflect vagus nerve-related challenges.
- **Anxiety and Mood Swings:** Chronic anxiety, mood swings, or sudden shifts in mood that seem disproportionate to the situation might be

influenced by the vagus nerve's impact on neurotransmitter balance.

- **Sensory Sensitivities:** Heightened sensitivity to light, sound, touch, or other sensory stimuli could signal vagus nerve disruptions affecting sensory processing.
- **Breathing Difficulties:** Shortness of breath, shallow breathing, or difficulty taking deep breaths might indicate vagus nerve involvement in respiratory control.
- **Chronic Inflammation:** Conditions characterized by chronic inflammation, such as autoimmune disorders, could suggest vagus nerve dysfunction, as this nerve plays a role in regulating inflammation.
- **Poor Stress Response:** If you find it challenging to recover from stress or if stress seems to affect you more intensely, the vagus nerve's role in managing stress responses could be a factor.
- **Reduced Ability to Focus:** If you struggle with maintaining attention and focus, the vagus nerve's influence on neurotransmitter balance and cognitive function could be implicated.
- **Social Engagement Difficulties:** The vagus nerve is tied to the body's "rest and digest" response, impacting social engagement. If you find social interactions draining or difficult, it might be connected to vagus nerve imbalances.

In addition to self-assessment, medical imaging tests like MRI and CT scans can be used to assess the nerves and surrounding structures. In addition, Nerve

Conduction Studies (NCS) and Electromyography (EMG) measure the electrical activity of nerves and muscles and can help identify nerve damage or dysfunction.

Vagus Nerve Stimulation

Techniques like deep breathing and mindfulness can help calm the vagus nerve. Yoga poses like the humble Downward Dog and relaxing Child's Pose can also help set things straight!

Additionally, there's chiropractic care. This holistic approach can indirectly impact the vagus nerve by ensuring spinal alignment and fostering an environment essential to vagus nerve health.

I can attest that vagus nerve stimulation can contribute to an overall sense of calm. Guided by an energy healer, I reclined on my back and engaged in a practice that involved gentle head and eye movements. With my face turned in one direction, I focused my gaze on a distant point in the opposite direction for approximately 30 seconds. I then repeated this process on both sides three times. Little did I know that this seemingly straightforward exercise would stimulate my vagus nerve and contribute to a sense of tranquility and balance I could feel instantly within my body.

A more intense form of stimulation involves a device approved by the Food and Drug Administration (FDA) to treat epilepsy and depression. The implantable vagus nerve stimulator works by sending stimulation to areas of the brain that lead to seizures and affect mood.

Whether you visit a neurologist, chiropractor, or holistic energy healer - if you suspect the vagus nerve could be contributing to your ADHD symptoms, I recommend seeking guidance from a professional. Let's now pivot our attention from neural routes to essential nutrients. In the next section, I'm going to show how vitamin and nutrient deficiencies can be a HUGE contributor to ADHD symptoms and quite the easy fix!

6

Oh, The IRONy

Vitamins and minerals aren't just building blocks for our body; they're essential for the smooth operation of our mind.

The Brain Needs Specific Nutrients For Optimal Functioning

Right at the heart of our brain's incredible capabilities, there's this intricate network of nutrients. These nutrients are the essential building blocks, energy sources, and catalysts that enable our brain cells to communicate, process information, and regulate our moods. Some of the top brain nutrients include

- **Omega-3 Fatty Acids**: These essential fats, found abundantly in fatty fish, flaxseeds, and walnuts, are integral for maintaining the structure of brain cell membranes and promoting optimal nerve function.
- **B Vitamins**: B vitamins, particularly B6, B9 (folate), and B12, are vital for neurotransmitter synthesis, helping regulate mood and cognitive function. Leafy greens, eggs, and fortified cereals are rich sources.
- **Antioxidants:** Vitamins C and E, along with minerals like selenium and zinc, act as powerful antioxidants, protecting brain cells from oxidative stress and inflammation.
- **Minerals:** Magnesium, iron, and zinc are crucial for neurotransmitter synthesis, nerve signaling, and oxygen delivery to brain cells.
- **Amino Acids:** Protein-rich foods provide the amino acids necessary for neurotransmitter production. Tryptophan, for instance, is a precursor to serotonin, a neurotransmitter that affects mood and sleep.
- **Choline:** This nutrient is a precursor to acetylcholine, a neurotransmitter that supports memory, learning, and muscle control. Eggs, liver, and soybeans are choline-rich foods.

- **Phospholipids:** Essential for cell membrane structure, phospholipids are found in foods like eggs and organ meats.
- **Vitamin D:** Beyond its role in bone health, vitamin D also influences brain function and development. Exposure to sunlight and fortified foods can help maintain adequate levels.
- **Iron:** This mineral is essential for oxygen transport to brain cells. Good sources include lean meats, beans, and fortified cereals.
- **Zinc:** Required for brain cell communication and neurotransmitter function, zinc can be found in meat, seafood, and legumes.
-

Identifying Deficiencies

Spotting the signs of a nutritional deficiency can be tricky. Symptoms can often overlap with various other health conditions. The Organic Acids Test (OAT), as mentioned in the gut health section, is a great way to measure vitamin and mineral deficiencies.

Your healthcare provider or nutrition coach should have access to this test and many others to give you a snapshot of your vitamin and mineral health.

Dietary Approach

The kitchen can be a pharmacy, with the foods we eat serving as medicine. When talking to clients about brain health, my rule of thumb is simple: avoid heavily processed foods and focus on REAL foods. Real food is food that comes from nature and does include meat.

Supplements

Sometimes, our body needs extra support to bridge the gap between what we eat and need. Consulting with your functional healthcare provider or nutrition coach is a great idea before starting a supplement plan because everyone processes vitamins differently.

Our experience with deficiencies

The OAT test revealed deficiencies in super important brain vitamins for my family, such as vitamin D, calcium, B12, & magnesium. When connected with a high-quality supplement through our natural health doctor, we saw a difference in all symptoms within two months. Unfortunately, if the deficiency is caused by malabsorption, or in our case - poor methylation because of genetic mutations, it can be a little more challenging to solve, but not impossible. Let's dig into that part now.

7
M*TH**F****R

MTHFR - I know what that abbreviation looks like, but it actually stands for something totally different: methylenetetrahydrofolate reductase!

WTF is MTHFR?

We all have the MTHFR gene in our DNA. We actually have two copies! One from our mother and one from our father. The MTHFR gene encodes our MTHFR enzymes to perform **a critical process called methylation**.

Methylation

Almost everything that enters the body gets converted into a usable form. This conversion process is called methylation.

Here are some examples of methylation that relate to brain health:

Folate (Vitamin B9) gets converted into its active form - 5-MTHF, for the body to use for cell growth, detoxification, hormone balance, cell growth, and, importantly, the health of neurotransmitters like dopamine, serotonin, and norepinephrine - all **regulating our mood!**

Methylation is also involved in the conversion of dopamine to norepinephrine, a critical step in the synthesis of adrenaline. This process allows the body to produce adrenaline when needed, such as during moments of stress, excitement, or danger, helping you **stay focused and ready to respond to challenges** or threats.

Dietary choline is converted into a compound called phosphocholine (PC). This chemical compound ensures cells can communicate, allowing **your memory, learning, and overall brain function to work better.**

Dirty Rotten Ancestors

Get this: In 1994, a scientist discovered two mutations of this gene. [1]

Now, somewhere between 40 & 50 percent of the US population have at least one MTHFR gene mutation.

So what's the big deal? Even one mutation could mean you may not get enough MTHFR enzyme action inside your body, leading to poor methylation!

Without proper methylation, you could be left depleted of chemical compounds and nutrients needed to allow your body and brain to function optimally! If the body cannot detox properly, you could also be stuck holding onto parasites, chemicals, mold, and other toxins like heavy metals. **All of this happily rolling out the red carpet for ADHD and in some cases - Autism!**

I found that one copy of my MTHFR gene has <u>one</u> of these mutations. If this mutation is the culprit to my previously mentioned issues, imagine someone having multiple mutations. What could that look like? It's a lot more severe than ADHD symptoms, I assume.

A quick web search resulted in a blog post from a medical doctor [2], spelling out some common symptoms of MTHFR Gene Mutation and poor methylation, and these include:

- ADHD (Attention Deficit Hyperactivity Disorder)
- Autism - This one makes sense as it is proven that people with autism have difficulties detoxing from heavy metals. [3] I haven't found any studies that show **everyone with autism** or a certain percentage of those with autism have an MTHFR gene mutation, but I would love to know if that's the case!
- Autoimmune disease and thyroid issues
- Cardiovascular disease
- Chronic fatigue
- Colon Cancer
- Digestive Issues, including IBS (Irritable Bowel Syndrome)
- Hormonal issues, including PCOS (Polycystic Ovary Syndrome)
- Migraines
- Schizophrenia

How to Discover if You Have an MTHFR Mutation

You can visit your healthcare provider to talk about testing options. Alternatively, you can order a DNA test online yourself.

Another option is a methylation pathway test, which analyzes five key methylation pathways, including cysteine, glycine, dopamine, serotonin, and of course methylation itself. Methylation pathways are also measured in the Organic Acids Test I mentioned before, but a DNA test may also interest you.

Your DNA can be very cool to look at, and it's how I found that I had the mutation - I even found that I'm more likely to like the taste of cilantro compared to some who think it tastes like soap! It's irrelevant, but it's still pretty dang cool to know.

The Good News: Our Genes Are Not Our Destiny!

Epigenetics, the study of gene expression, says that diet, exercise, exposure to toxins, and medications can influence our genes and traits. Nutrition, in particular, influences genetic expression. This means certain genes can be turned "on" or "off" like a light switch, depending on your eating!

There are some steps you can take to decrease complications from having an MTHFR gene mutation and aid your methylation process:

Eat Clean & Green To Support Detoxification

Because poor methylation contributes to reduced detoxification, supporting your body's natural detoxification is important. Consume organic folate-rich foods such as dark leafy greens, asparagus, calf's liver, broccoli, cauliflower, beets, celery, avocados, and lentils! Fill your diet with a healthy amount of vitamin B6 foods such as spinach, bell peppers, garlic, tuna, bananas, & cabbage.

Supplements

Pre-methylated B vitamins: For those with MTHFR mutations, folate must be pre-methylated (5 MTHF) to bypass methylation.

Non-pre-methylated B vitamins are a waste for someone who cannot convert folic acid into folate and then into 5-MTHF. In theory, folic acid, an artificial chemical, could be dangerous for those struggling with methylation, causing folic acid buildup.
Other supplements that support methylation include Magnesium, Vitamin D, and Glutathione.

Manage Stress With Lifestyle Changes

An imbalance of neurotransmitter levels is more likely in those with MTHFR mutations. High levels of stress can worsen poor methylation symptoms. Try discovering some activities that help you unwind, stay grounded, and decompress.

Decrease Alcohol Intake

Alcohol intake increases detoxification demands on the liver. Methylation processes may already be impaired in those with MTHFR gene mutations, so only consuming alcohol in moderation or not at all is recommended by some doctors.

Not all gene variants and mutations are cut from the same cloth; some may carry more weight than others. If MTHFR concerns are on your radar, you may want to team up with a healthcare professional with the know-how to steer you through the right tests and game plan. What you're looking for here is a medical geneticist or genetic counselor. Some health coaches can even assist you with finding the answers you need.

I mentioned being stuck with heavy metals if the body has difficulty detoxifying them due to poor methylation. Next, we'll look at some of those metals and explore the havoc each one can create! We'll examine how heavy metal toxicity can mimic many disorders, such as depression, ASD, ADHD, and anxiety.

8
Toxic Heavy Metals

We're getting into some real-world shit here: **heavy metal**, and not the good kind like Metallica or Slipknot; I'm talkin' about the low-key risks of lead exposure and the nasty chemicals lurking in public water systems. Plus, there's this whole thing with sneaky toxic heavy metals in the air we breathe. I will explain how all this stuff might mess with our brains and maybe even have a hand in ADHD & ASD symptoms.

Toxic exposure isn't too picky; it can affect anyone. But don't forget about MTHFR. That's still on the radar because it can be even worse for folks who can't detoxify well.

Lead

Lead, a heavy metal that was once commonly used in products like paint and gasoline, has been linked to severe cognitive problems, particularly in children. Paint fragments, dust, and plumbing systems, soil, potable water, and atmospheric pollutants can also contribute to lead exposure.[4] Numerous studies have provided compelling evidence that exposure to lead during early life, even at low levels, is linked to decreased attention span and decreased academic performance in children.[5]" Another 2016 study showed that even lead exposure among adults at levels previously considered safe resulted in impairment of certain cognitive abilities. [6]

No level of lead exposure can be deemed safe for human consumption. [7]

Lead is a sneaky little shit; when it enters the body, it can be disguised as a mineral like calcium, which the body then absorbs and distributes throughout various tissues, including the brain. Once in the brain, it interferes with the normal functioning of neurons and disrupts the connections between brain cells and neurotransmitters.

Even at low levels, lead exposure at a young age can hinder the growth and organization of brain cells, leading to deficits in cognitive function, attention, and behavior regulation like ADHD. [8]

Mercury

Mercury exposure can occur through consuming seafood, receiving dental amalgams (mercury fillings), polluted air, and even some vaccines.

Mercury, a potent neurotoxin, can enter the body and directly traverse the blood-brain barrier building up within brain tissue and the spinal cord. Once built up, it can trigger an inflammatory response in the nervous system. Inflammation in the brain and spinal cord will then contribute to tissue damage and play a role in developing neurodegenerative conditions and cognitive impairment.

Furthermore, research shows that prenatal mercury exposure correlates with ADHD symptoms in children. [8]

A review of 44 studies established that mercury levels are notably elevated in the blood and brains of individuals with autism (ASD).[9] It is important to note that the conclusion of this review determined that detoxification mechanisms are impaired in ASD patients, which could cause mercury accumulation in their blood and brain. Is MTHFR the cause? I'd sure love to know!

Hang tight because here is where I cross a very controversial line. The debate over vaccines states that although there is a small amount of mercury in certain vaccines, it is a different type of mercury that the body is able to eliminate. My concern lies with the fact that people, over 40% of the population, potentially have poor methylation - some worse than others, depending on the extent of potential gene mutations. Wouldn't that make them the exception? Wouldn't a parent want to know about methylation health prior to deciding on an injection containing heavy metals?

Aluminum

Aluminum is everywhere, from deodorant to cookware and most canned goods. Aluminum can even be found in antacids and added to vaccines to enhance the body's immune response to the vaccine's antigens. The FDA claims that aluminum exposure is safe in small amounts; however, in recent years, there has been more focus on the public debate about the neurotoxic effect of aluminum and its potential carcinogenic effect. Elevated aluminum content has been found in the brains of individuals with Alzheimer's, yet it's still unclear whether it is the cause or effect. Aluminum has been shown to decrease attention, learning, and memory in adults with above-normal exposure.[10]

Manganese

Manganese, a natural heavy metal, in small amounts, is essential for the body. It contributes to things like metabolizing carbohydrates, bone growth, and wound healing. Manganese can be found in green leafy vegetables, tea, and legumes.

Too much of a good thing is not always a good thing. Manganese toxicity has been linked to ADHD, lack of intellectual function, and behavioral problems.[11]

Toxic exposure can result from inhaling a lot of manganese dust or from elevated manganese levels in public drinking water. Steer clear of public drinking water if it has any kind of brownish tint to avoid manganese toxicity.

Fluoride

Fluoride, while not a heavy metal, is worth mentioning here. It is a naturally occurring chemical compound that contains the element fluorine. It is commonly added to public water supplies in small amounts as a means to help prevent tooth decay and promote oral health. Additionally, fluoride is often found in dental products like toothpaste and mouthwash. However, ingestion of fluoride, especially during critical stages of development, can potentially lead to adverse health effects.

Drawn from a body of evidence found in various human studies spanning different populations, The National Toxicology Program (NTP)'s review of the correlation between exposure to fluoride and its potential impacts on neurodevelopment and cognitive well-being led to the conclusion that fluoride could be regarded as a cognitive neurodevelopment risk for humans.[12]

In addition, current evidence from a variety of studies indicates that fluoride exposure may lead to behavioral alterations, cognitive impairment, and psychosomatic issues. [13]

Step 1. Reduce Exposure

Reducing exposure to heavy metals involves making conscious choices to minimize contact with sources of these toxins. Here are some steps you can take:

Dietary Choices

Choose organic produce whenever possible to reduce exposure to pesticides and chemicals. Check the EPA's Dirty Dozen list for foods to avoid.

Consume a variety of foods to avoid excessive exposure to a specific heavy metal.

Opt for wild-caught fish low in mercury, such as salmon or sardines.
Be cautious with seafood known to be higher in mercury, such as shark, swordfish, and king mackerel.

Avoid farmed fish, food with additives, and alcohol.

Water Quality

Use a water filter that is certified to remove heavy metals, such as lead and mercury, from drinking water.

If you have a private well, ensure regular water testing for heavy metals.

Household Products

Choose lead-free paints, especially if you have young children.

Avoid using ceramic cookware that may contain lead glazes.

Use stainless steel, glass, or ceramic containers for food storage instead of plastic or aluminum.

Personal Care and Cosmetics

Use personal care products and cosmetics that are free from heavy metals, artificial colors, and fragrances.

Check ingredients' labels and avoid products containing lead, mercury, or other harmful chemicals.

Home Environment

Keep your home well-ventilated to reduce indoor air pollution.

Regularly dust and clean your home to minimize exposure to dust containing heavy metals.

Occupational Precautions

If your work involves exposure to heavy metals, follow safety protocols and use protective gear.

Wash your hands and change clothes after working in environments with potential heavy metal exposure.

Avoid Tobacco and Secondhand Smoke

Smoking and exposure to secondhand smoke can introduce heavy metals into the body.

Step 2. Test for Heavy Metals

If you think heavy metal toxicity could be at the root of your ADHD symptoms or throwing your general health for a loop, reach out to a specialist for testing and guidance on eliminating the metals from your body. There are some great heavy metal detox experts online. They ship the test to you, you return the sample and then follow up with a virtual consultation about your results.

Step 3. Heavy Metal Detox

Here are some general steps to consider for supporting your body's natural detoxification processes:

Nutrient Support

Ensure your diet includes nutrient-rich foods that support detoxification.

Incorporate sulfur-rich foods such as garlic and onions, which assist your liver in detoxifying heavy metals like lead & arsenic.

Embrace a diet abundant in vitamin C - Fruits and vegetables loaded with this vital nutrient possess antioxidant properties that combat the harm stemming from heavy metal toxicity. Elevate your vitamin C intake by consuming citrus fruits, leafy greens, an assortment of berries, nutrient-packed broccoli, cruciferous vegetables, and kiwi, papaya, guava, and bell peppers. Supplement with vitamin C if necessary.

Consume plenty of Omega-3 fats and Fiber with foods such as avocado, flax & chia seeds, legumes, berries, and fatty fish (wild-caught salmon is a good choice- avoid fish with high mercury).

Hydration

Drink plenty of clean, filtered water to support kidney function and help flush toxins from your body. Avoid tap water if possible, or add an in-home filter.

Bone broth plays a multifaceted role in your well-being. Not only does it aid in maintaining hydration, but it also supplies essential minerals while bolstering liver health through its glutathione content. Furthermore, the amino acids in bone broth contribute to fortifying your organs.

Sauna Therapy

Infrared saunas or regular saunas can help promote sweating, which can aid in the elimination of toxins through the skin.

Colon Health

A healthy colon is essential for eliminating waste and toxins. Consider incorporating fiber-rich foods and probiotics into your diet.

Liver Support

The liver plays a key role in detoxification. Support its function with foods like artichokes, dandelion greens, and turmeric.

Manage Stress

Chronic stress can hinder the body's detoxification processes—practice stress-reduction techniques like meditation, deep breathing, and yoga.

Natural Detoxifiers

Herbs and spices with anti-inflammatory and antioxidant properties, such as basil, parsley, oregano, rosemary, thyme, ginger, turmeric, cinnamon, and cilantro, have the potential to aid in the elimination of heavy metals. Among these, cilantro stands out as a valuable herb for detoxification. Alongside other green herbs and plants, cilantro can reduce the accumulation of heavy metals like mercury and lead within the body.

Supplements To Consider

Vitamin C: At a daily dosage of 3000 milligrams, vitamin C is an antioxidant, mitigating the impact of free radicals.

Liposomal Glutathione: At a daily dosage of 100mg, Glutathione is like a superhero molecule in our bodies. It's a powerful antioxidant that helps protect our cells from damage and supports our overall health. When it comes to heavy metal detox, glutathione helps grab onto harmful metals and safely escort them out of our system.

Probiotics (Soil-Based): Incorporating soil-based probiotics at a strength of 50 billion units once daily can enhance gut detoxification and bolster the immune system. Some common strains of soil-based probiotics include Bacillus subtilis, Bacillus coagulans, and Bacillus Clausii.

Essential Minerals: A complete mineral complex is ideal for use when mineral replenishment is desired. As mentioned above, heavy metals can deplete the body of natural minerals. Mineral replacement is highly recommended if you suspect heavy metal toxicity.

Vitamin B Complex (Pre-Methylated): Vitamin B complex can benefit heavy metal detoxification. B vitamins play important roles in supporting your body's detoxification processes. Vitamin B6, in particular, can help enhance the production of glutathione, a powerful antioxidant that aids in detoxification.

Activated Charcoal: Activated charcoal is like a natural sponge for toxins, including heavy metals. Taking activated charcoal binds to these harmful substances in your digestive tract, preventing them from being absorbed into your body.

Chlorella: The intake of chlorella, a green algae, at 1-4 grams per day (equivalent to about 4-8 capsules daily) acts as a natural chelator to remove heavy metals such as lead and mercury. Chlorella can be consumed in powder or tablet form.

Consult a Healthcare Professional

It's important to note that heavy metal detoxification can release stored toxins into the bloodstream, potentially causing adverse reactions. Therefore, I recommend working with a specialist who can tailor a detox plan to your needs, monitor your progress, and ensure your safety throughout the process.

For more intensive detoxification, such as chelation therapy (a medical procedure to remove heavy metals), consult a healthcare provider experienced in this area.

Potential Side Effects of a Heavy Metal Detox

Symptoms could worsen before they get better, given during a detox, metals are released back into the body before being eliminated. Initially, you may experience the following: bloating and gas, nausea or vomiting, diarrhea or constipation, headaches, a skin rash, changes in appetite, low energy, and a metallic or sour taste in the mouth.

I recommend detoxing slowly and gradually by making small changes over time. Aggressive detoxification can lead to worsened ADHD symptoms and the symptoms listed above.

Women who are contemplating pregnancy should be aware of their heavy metal levels. Metal toxicity can hinder the development of newborns. Suppose a woman has been diagnosed with elevated levels of heavy metals, such as mercury. In that case, it's advisable to postpone any planned pregnancies by a few months while working to restore normal levels to promote a healthier pregnancy and childbirth. Remember that the human body has its own natural detoxification mechanisms, and supporting those through a healthy lifestyle and diet is often the best approach.
Detoxing should not be done as a quick fix but rather as a long-term commitment to overall well-being.

Our focus will now pivot to a subject equally relevant. In the upcoming chapter, we'll look at food-induced ADHD, where you will find out - you are what you eat.

9
Food-Induced B.S.

Let's face it: we're not eating the same foods today as our great-grandmothers. Food choices have become complex, and conflicting diet advice hits us from every angle. Food choices can be overwhelming, and worse - choosing foods or food-like products that don't agree with our bodies can jack up our physical and mental health pretty damn bad. What we eat can screw up our mental clarity, focus, attention, and overall brain function.

The Cognitive Culprits of Food

Classic ADHD and mental health symptoms can result from toxic food substances, allergies, and intolerance. Here are a few symptoms of food-induced health problems and ADHD:

Brain Fog: A feeling of mental confusion, difficulty concentrating, and reduced clarity in thought processes.

Attention Challenges: Struggles with maintaining focus, staying on task, and easily getting distracted.

Impulsive Behavior: Difficulty controlling impulses, leading to quick decisions and actions without much thought.

Mood Swings: Rapid shifts in mood, including irritability, anxiety, and even depressive feelings.

Energy Fluctuations: Experiencing crashes in energy levels, leading to periods of fatigue and lack of vitality.

Hyperactivity: Restlessness, fidgeting, and an excess of energy that can interfere with calm and focused behavior.

Sleep Disturbances: Disruptions in sleep patterns, including difficulty falling or staying asleep.

Digestive Discomfort: Gastrointestinal issues like bloating, gas, and discomfort that can indirectly impact cognitive function.

Anxiety: Persistent feelings of unease, worry, and nervousness that can affect focus and decision-making.

Depression: Overwhelming sadness, loss of interest, and low energy that impacts cognitive abilities.

Intolerance & Allergies

Dietary Intolerance

Food intolerance is the body's inability to digest certain foods or substances. When a person consumes a food to which they are intolerant, it can trigger symptoms like inflammation and changes in gut bacteria, impacting the production of neurotransmitters that play a crucial role in regulating mood, attention, and behavior.

Dietary Allergies

A food allergy is different. It is an immune system response. The body mistakenly identifies specific proteins in the food as harmful.

When a food allergy activates the immune system, it can lead to inflammation, affecting various parts of the body, including the brain. Neuroinflammation, which results from immune activation in the brain, has been linked to cognitive impairments, mood disorders, and attention difficulties that resemble ADHD symptoms.

The release of histamine can also disrupt neurotransmitter balance in the brain. Neurotransmitters like serotonin and dopamine play key roles in regulating mood, focus, and behavior.

Imbalances in these neurotransmitters can lead to symptoms such as irritability, impulsivity, and difficulty concentrating – all of which can resemble ADHD-like behaviors.

Our Food Is Changing

By now, we've all heard it:

"Back in my day, ADHD wasn't such a common thing, or we didn't know anyone with celiac disease or autism."

Guess what? There might be a nugget of truth there. Those yesteryears had something rare - real food.

Looking at the rise of processed foods, the reign of industrial farming, the debut of GMOs, and the not-so-pretty picture of pesticides, you can see what we put on our plates and how we live our lives has shifted dramatically!

If we could peek back fifty years, we'd see that our food choices and lifestyles were a whole different ball game. And that, my friend, might just be a piece of the puzzle when we're talking about the evolving story of ADHD and Autism.

Modern Wheat Is An Asshole

Once a staple of sustenance, wheat has undergone substantial transformation due to modern agricultural practices. Today's wheat bears little resemblance to its ancestors, and this shift has been implicated in the rise of gluten sensitivity.

Wheat strains have been altered, bred, and hybridized in the quest for greater yield and efficiency. These modifications have given rise to what's now commonly known as modern wheat. This wheat version contains higher gluten content than its predecessors, making it more elastic and desirable for baking and food production.

But there's another twist to the tale: Desiccation, or "killing" the wheat before harvest. Many wheat crops are treated with glyphosate-based herbicides to expedite the harvesting process and ensure uniform ripening. Glyphosate is an herbicide commonly found in products like Roundup. It's intended to speed up the wheat drying, making it easier to harvest. One concern is that this roundup lurks its way into the food system.

For many, the immune system reacts to these altered proteins in ways that manifest as gluten-related disorders, such as celiac disease or non-celiac gluten sensitivity.
In the case of celiac disease, the immune system's response to gluten can significantly damage the lining

of the small intestine. This damage can impair nutrient absorption, potentially causing deficiencies in essential vitamins and minerals that are crucial to cognitive function. For instance, iron, zinc, and B vitamin nutrient deficiencies have been associated with cognitive challenges and behavioral issues that overlap with ADHD symptoms.

On the other hand, non-celiac gluten sensitivity does not involve the same level of damage to the gut lining as celiac disease. However, it can still lead to various symptoms, including neurological and behavioral issues. Some individuals with non-celiac gluten sensitivity may experience brain fog, mood swings, and difficulty concentrating, all of which are common features of ADHD.

Fake AF

"Fake food" is a term I often use to describe processed or highly manipulated food-like products that often contain artificial ingredients, additives, and preservatives. These substances are added to enhance flavor, color, texture, and shelf life but lack the nutritional value of whole, natural foods. Fake foods are typically high in sugar, unhealthy fats, and artificial chemicals while low in essential nutrients, vitamins, and minerals. Consuming a diet rich in fake foods can negatively impact health, contributing to various health issues such as obesity, diabetes, heart disease, and cognitive challenges.

Consuming fake food can leave you feeling hungry and unsatisfied despite consuming calories. This happens because these foods are often low in essential nutrients, fiber, and protein, which are key components to brain health and feeling full. When you eat heavily processed fake foods, your body may receive a burst of calories from sugars and unhealthy fats. Still, it lacks the nourishment it needs to maintain balanced energy levels and feel satisfied. As a result, your body's hunger signals remain active, and you may find yourself craving more food shortly after eating. The rapid spikes and crashes in blood sugar can further exacerbate feelings of hunger and reduced cognitive functioning, as your body is in a state of survival.

An influential study published in The Lancet, involving nearly 300 children, demonstrated that these additives could trigger symptoms of hyperactivity in both younger and older children.
In addition to all that bullshit, these foods contain some super dangerous crap that the FDA should not approve. As a matter of fact, in some countries, these ingredients are prohibited!

For example, if you look at the ingredients of Mac-N-Cheese in the United States vs. the United Kingdom by the same company, you will notice there are far fewer ingredients in the UK. Below is an ingredient list of the same brand but in different countries.

United State Mac -N- Cheese

Enriched Macaroni Product (Wheat Flour, Niacin, Ferrous Sulfate [Iron], Thiamin Mononitrate [Vitamin B1], Riboflavin [Vitamin B2], Folic Acid), Cheese Sauce Mix (Whey, Modified Food Starch, Whey Protein Concentrate, Cheddar Cheese [Milk, Cheese Culture, Salt, Enzymes], Salt, Calcium Carbonate, Potassium Chloride, Contains Less Than 2% of Parmesan Cheese [Part-Skim Milk, Cheese Culture, Salt, Enzymes, Dried Buttermilk, Sodium Tripolyphosphate, Blue Cheese [Milk, Cheese Culture, Salt, Enzymes], Sodium Phosphate, Medium Chain Triglycerides, Cream, Citric Acid, Lactic Acid, Enzymes, Yellow 5, Yellow 6).

United Kingdom Mac -N- Cheese

Macaroni (Durum Wheat Semolina), Cheese (10%), Whey Powder (from milk), Lactose, Salt, Emulsifying Salts (E339, E341), Colors (Paprika Extract, Beta-Carotene)

FUN FACT: CHILDREN ARE LESS LIKELY TO BE DIAGNOSED WITH ADHD IN THE UK THAN THEY ARE IN THE US!

Artificial food coloring and food dyes are also gaining traction as potential culprits for behavior and mood issues in children and adults!

Some parents and doctors ^14 have found fascinating connections between food dyes and specific behaviors such as horrible temper tantrums when exposed to yellow dyes, irritability or fatigue when exposed to blue, and manic episodes when exposed to green dyes.

Research shows children with diagnosed ADHD can improve significantly on a dye-free diet.^15

Blood Sugar Imbalance

We can't forget highly addictive sugar! Blood sugar imbalance occurs when the levels of glucose (sugar) in the bloodstream fluctuate significantly and erratically. This can lead to a range of physical and cognitive symptoms that can mimic ADHD too.

Here's how blood sugar imbalance can resemble ADHD symptoms:

Inattention and Poor Focus: When blood sugar levels are too high or too low, the brain may not receive a consistent supply of glucose, its primary energy source. This can result in difficulties with concentration, focus, and attention, similar to the distractibility and inattention often seen in individuals with ADHD.

Hyperactivity and Impulsivity: Blood sugar spikes followed by crashes can lead to sudden bursts of energy followed by periods of fatigue. This can manifest as hyperactivity and impulsive behavior, resembling the restlessness and impulsivity associated with ADHD.

Mood Swings: Rapid fluctuations in blood sugar levels can impact mood regulation. Spikes and crashes in glucose can lead to irritability, mood swings, and emotional instability, also common traits seen in individuals with ADHD.

Difficulty with Executive Functioning: Blood sugar imbalance can impair the brain's executive functions, such as planning, organization, decision-making, and problem-solving. These functions are already compromised in individuals with ADHD, so blood sugar fluctuations can exacerbate these challenges.

Cognitive Fog (brain fog): Fluctuations in blood sugar can lead to cognitive fog, mental confusion, and difficulty processing information. This can mirror the cognitive challenges, brain fog, and mental clarity issues often associated with ADHD.

Restlessness and Agitation: Blood sugar imbalances can lead to feelings of restlessness, jitteriness, and agitation, resembling the physical restlessness and agitation sometimes observed in individuals with ADHD.

In addition to blood sugar spikes and crashes, fructose (a molecule in sugar) has a biochemical profile very similar to alcohol and can be highly addictive.

The third big issue is that our bodies have limited capacity to metabolize refined sugar, so it speeds through the digestive process, causing blood sugar levels to skyrocket and making you feel hungry again quickly, leading to further sugar cravings.

Fruit sugar is digested slower due to the higher fiber content. If you have a sweet tooth that won't subside, it's better to turn to fruit, but I wouldn't recommend starting your day with it.

It's scary that one of the most dangerous foods for health, weight, and brain function is marketed mainly for either celebrations or the most important meal of the day: breakfast. If I had known then what I know now, I would have never allowed my kids to start the day with muffins, pop-tarts, pancakes, or sugary cereals. We now opt for foods high in protein and healthy fats.

Suppose you suspect that blood sugar fluctuations are contributing to ADHD-like symptoms. In that case, it's a good idea to discuss fasting blood sugar tests or glucose tolerance tests with your provider, which can provide a clearer picture of your blood sugar dynamics and potential connections to your symptoms. Don't settle for an A1C test. This test primarily measures your average blood sugar levels over the past 2 to 3 months, providing insight into your overall blood sugar control. While an A1C test is a valuable tool for diagnosing and monitoring diabetes and prediabetes, it may not be as sensitive to short-term fluctuations in blood sugar that can lead to ADHD-like symptoms due to blood sugar imbalance.

The Power of an ADHD Elimination Diet

An elimination diet is a period (usually a few weeks) where you remove all known ADHD trigger foods from your diet, then gradually introduce each food one at a time to see how the body and mind react.

A growing body of research proves food-induced ADHD, highlighting the power of an elimination diet. The Dutch conducted a study and observed that a highly restricted diet led to significant and substantial behavioral improvements in children with ADHD and oppositional defiant disorder (ODD). The children's diet during this study consisted mainly of rice, turkey, lamb, vegetables, fruits, tea, pear juice, and water.

Most importantly, they avoided milk products, wheat, sugar products, food additives, and artificial colors.

Remarkably, the study's results demonstrated that approximately 85% of the children who participated fully saw an improvement of 50% or more, no longer meeting the criteria for ADHD.

Additionally, about 67% of the participants with ODD no longer met the criteria for that condition. These findings were reaffirmed when the study was repeated, yielding similar positive outcomes. Another study published in the European Journal of Pediatrics, which employed the same diet, also reported enhancements in physical symptoms like headaches and bellyaches and improvements in sleep patterns.

Before starting an elimination diet, it's a good idea to consult with a professional, such as a registered dietitian, nutritionist, health coach, or doctor specializing in nutrition, to ensure it's safe and appropriate for your needs. You also want to ensure that you are not putting your body at risk by eliminating vitamins and nutrients. Here's a basic elimination diet outline to get you started.

Choose an Elimination Plan

Determine which foods to eliminate: Based on your symptoms and suspicions, decide which foods you want to stop. Common culprits of food-induced ADHD symptoms can include gluten, dairy, soy, corn, artificial additives, artificial colors, and most definitely added sugars.

Research & Plan

Look for foods you can eat while avoiding the eliminated foods. Paleo foods are a good place to start. This will help you maintain a balanced and nutritious diet.

Plan your meals: Create a meal plan that includes a variety of foods to ensure you're getting all the essential nutrients. Planning and meal prepping will help you stay the course.

Start the Elimination Phase

Eliminate the chosen foods: Completely remove the identified trigger foods from your diet for a specified period, typically around 2-4 weeks. Keep a journal to track your symptoms throughout this phase.

Document any changes in your physical and mental health during the elimination phase. Pay close attention to improvements or changes in ADHD-like symptoms.

Reintroduction Phase

Introduce one food at a time. After the elimination phase, start reintroducing one eliminated food at a time. Give this food 3-4 days before introducing another. Document every day your mood changes, brain fog, irritability, etc.

Women should avoid testing new foods or starting an elimination diet during the luteal phase of their menstruation cycle as this phase involves a decline in estrogen and progesterone levels, which can lead to mood changes, irritability, and fatigue. It may be beneficial to do several elimination diets for a few months with different foods.

Observe reactions: As you reintroduce each food, monitor for any changes in symptoms. Keep notes on how you feel physically and mentally after consuming the reintroduced food.

Symptoms can occur within a few minutes or up to 72 hours later. If you notice a problem, stop consuming that food immediately. Reactions to foods can include but are not limited to:

- Brain fog, lack of motivation, restlessness
- Memory issues
- Imbalanced mood (anxiety, irritability, depression)
- Congestion
- Sleep problems or fatigue

- Aches & Pain: Joints, Stomach, Muscles, Headaches, etc.
- Skin changes
- Changes in digestion and bowel functioning
- Hyperactivity

Plan for the Future

Develop a sustainable diet: Based on your findings, work with a professional to create a sustainable eating plan that addresses your dietary needs and minimizes symptom triggers.

This process can take time and patience, but it can provide valuable insights into how your diet may affect your overall health and well-being.

It is important to note that I define nutrition as anything that feeds your body, spirit, and mind. Let's talk about what doesn't feed our minds so well.

10
Well, That Hurt

Trauma is a psychological and emotional response to an event or series of events that are distressing, harmful, or threatening to an individual's physical or emotional well-being. Trauma can result from many experiences, such as accidents, abuse, violence, natural disasters, losing a loved one, or other life-threatening situations. It often overwhelms a person's ability to cope and may lead to a range of emotional, psychological, and physical symptoms.

There are different types of trauma, including

- **Physical Trauma**. Caused by accidents, injuries, or medical procedures that result in physical harm or pain.
- **Emotional or Psychological Trauma**. Arises from distressing emotional experiences, such as abuse, neglect, or witnessing traumatic events.
- **Developmental Trauma**. Occurs during childhood and can lead to long-lasting emotional difficulties.
- **Post-Traumatic Stress Disorder (PTSD):** A specific type of trauma characterized by persistent and distressing symptoms following a traumatic event, such as flashbacks, nightmares, and severe anxiety.

The impact of trauma can vary from person to person. While some individuals may recover with time and support, others may require professional assistance and therapy to cope with and heal from the effects of trauma.
Traumatic experiences can have the power to reshape the way our minds work. These experiences can tinker with neural pathways, tweaking attention spans, memory recall, and emotional regulation.

The Trauma - ADHD Link

The remnants of trauma have an uncanny resemblance to the symptoms of ADHD. Hyperactivity, impulsivity, concentration challenges, and emotional roller coasters are all on the table. Imagine someone who's been through a traumatic event, finding it nearly impossible to sit still. It's not because they're casually disinterested; it's more like a jolted nervous system struggling to find equilibrium.

Emotional triggers from trauma can transform calm waters into category 5 storms of mood swings and sudden outbursts.

Coping With Trauma

In the wake of trauma, humans build up a wall of armor to cope. This strategy helps us escape the seas of emotions and haunting memories. The problem is, that while protective, this suppression can mimic the very symptoms of ADHD.

Imagine someone using avoidance as their shield against traumatic reminders. This can make them appear inattentive or easily distracted, yet they're just safeguarding themselves from a whirlwind of emotions. Dissociation, another common response to trauma, can make it seem like someone is drifting off into space when, in reality, they're managing overwhelming distress.

In addition, hypervigilance, or constant scanning of surroundings for danger, can look like a distraction.

Trauma-causing ADHD makes total sense, right? Well, here's where I shake things up. What about ADHD symptoms causing trauma? What an endless cycle of hell, am I right?

The Bidirectional Relationship

I CAN TESTIFY THAT ADHD SYMPTOMS THEMSELVES CAN BE TRAUMATIC AF.

Living a life with unmanaged symptoms like impulsivity, recklessness, and struggles with organization can put us in risky situations, potentially resulting in traumatic events or consequences.

Being labeled "a bad kid" and constantly ridiculed can be incredibly traumatic.

Pushing away friends and loved ones due to distractions, interrupting, and, like me: hyper-focusing to solve this problem can have traumatic effects.

Seek Help Today

As you can see, trauma can mirror ADHD symptoms, while ADHD traits can sometimes fuel the flames of traumatic experiences. Acknowledging these dynamics and seeking tailored support from a professional as soon as possible can pave the way toward healing and minimizing damage.

Trauma-focused and cognitive-behavioral therapy (CBT) offers tools to process traumatic events, cultivate healthy coping mechanisms, and manage ADHD symptoms. Alongside treatment, creating a nurturing environment that values emotional expression, fosters open communication, and practices empathy can be a cornerstone of healing.

Trauma is no joke. It can seriously impact your mental health. If you or someone you know is having thoughts of suicide, seek help immediately by calling the National Suicide & Crisis Hotline (Dial 988), dialing 911, or going to your nearest hospital.

11
You Can Relax Now
You're Safe

"Fight, flight, or freeze" is a natural and instinctual response that humans and animals experience when faced with a threat or a stressful situation. It's a physiological and psychological reaction that prepares the body to respond to danger.

Here's what each of these responses entails:

- **Fight:** When an individual perceives a threat, the "fight" response involves a surge of adrenaline and increased heart rate. This prepares the person to confront the threat head-on and engage in self-defense or take action to protect themselves or others.

- **Flight:** The "flight" response is characterized by the instinct to escape or avoid the threat. In this mode, the body releases adrenaline, increasing alertness and energy. It's an evolutionary survival mechanism to remove oneself from a dangerous situation quickly.

- **Freeze**: In some situations, a person might enter a "freeze" state instead of fighting or fleeing. During this response, the body becomes immobilized, and the individual may feel paralyzed with fear. This can happen when the person perceives neither fighting nor fleeing is a viable option. The freeze response can also serve as a way to hide from predators.

These responses are regulated by the sympathetic nervous system, which activates the body to respond to threats, and the parasympathetic nervous system, which helps the body relax after the threat has passed.

Fight or flight is a pretty cool mechanism when you need to kick ass or run for your life, but not required when facing work-related stress, social anxiety, or other emotionally challenging experiences.
What happens when we can't escape this defense mechanism, and we're caught in a loop of living in this state? When the body cannot return to homeostasis, chronic stress takes over.
Unfortunately, chronic stress doesn't just end when the stressor does. Our bodies can stay in this heightened state for prolonged periods, leading to a cascade of adverse effects on cognitive function. Our ability to concentrate diminishes, memory becomes fuzzy, and decision-making becomes clouded. It's like trying to focus on a task while a blaring alarm goes off in the background—nearly impossible.

Here are some symptoms of chronic stress that mimic ADHD.

Impaired Focus and Attention: Chronic stress can lead to difficulty sustaining attention and focusing on tasks. People experiencing chronic stress may find it hard to concentrate due to their mental preoccupation with stressors.

Forgetfulness: Chronic stress can result in forgetfulness and difficulty remembering important details, appointments, and tasks. Chronic stress may contribute to a scattered mind, leading to memory lapses.

Impulsivity: Impulsive behaviors, such as acting without thinking and making quick decisions, can be a common feature of chronic stress.

Emotional Dysregulation: Living in fight or flight mode can lead to mood swings, irritability, and emotional volatility. Chronic stress can amplify emotional reactions.

Fatigue and Exhaustion: Stress-related overthinking and worry can lead to mental fatigue.

Poor Time Management: Stress may cause a sense of urgency and difficulty in prioritizing tasks.

Physical Symptoms: Chronic stress can manifest in physical symptoms such as muscle tension, headaches, and gastrointestinal discomfort - some of the same symptoms seen in people with diagnosed ADHD.

As you can see, the parallels between the fight or flight response and ADHD-like symptoms are striking. When our brains are constantly on high alert, our cognitive resources are diverted from higher-level thinking and problem-solving. Cognitive Behavioral Therapy can help you escape living in survival mode, but here are some steps you can take yourself to manage stress.

Managing Chronic Stress

Mindfulness and relaxation practices provide a powerful toolkit for reining in the fight or flight response. We can reprogram our bodies' automatic reactions by learning to stay present, acknowledge our stressors without judgment, and practice deep breathing.

Incorporating Stress-Reducing Activities into Daily Life & Creating A Calm Environment

Managing stress doesn't mean eliminating it—after all, life will always throw challenges our way. However, we can build resilience and create a buffer against chronic stress by weaving stress-reducing activities into our daily routines. Whether it's a 10-minute meditation, a stroll in nature, or engaging in a hobby you love, these moments of reprieve can make a world of difference.

Our surroundings significantly influence our stress levels. Creating spaces that promote relaxation and well-being can help us find solace even in chaos. Consider soft lighting, soothing colors, and comforting textures to create an oasis of calm. Additionally, self-care isn't just a buzzword—it's essential. Treating yourself with kindness and compassion can provide a steady anchor when life's storms rage.

If you suspect you or someone you know is experiencing chronic stress, seeking professional evaluation is crucial for accurate diagnosis and effective management. A healthcare provider can help determine the underlying causes and develop a tailored plan for addressing the specific challenges in children and adults.

12

Seriously, Get Some Rest.

The land of dreams has a profound connection to our cognitive functions, and a lack of quality sleep can sometimes result in attention challenges, restlessness, and more.

Lack of adequate sleep doesn't just leave us tired; it can lead to a cascade of cognitive challenges that mimic the symptoms associated with ADHD. When sleep is compromised, our brain's executive functions take a hit. Impulsivity can surge to the forefront, tempting us into crappy decisions. Focus goes out the window. Finally, emotional stability becomes shaky, causing us to overreact to the slightest triggers.

Many neural processes take place while we are snoozing. Memories are consolidated, new information is processed, and our mental garden is pruned of unnecessary connections, making space for fresh insights. However, our brain takes a hit when our relationship with the Sandman turns rocky.

Sleep disorders

Sleep apnea, insomnia, and restless leg syndrome can disrupt the quality and quantity of sleep. Sleep apnea causes repeated interruptions in breathing during sleep, leading to fragmented rest and daytime sleepiness, which can be mistaken for ADHD. Similarly, insomnia can impair attention and concentration due to sleep deprivation. If you suspect that sleep issues might be contributing to ADHD - get it checked out ASAP!

Mind-Body Practices For Better Sleep

Meditation, deep breathing exercises, and progressive muscle relaxation can help alleviate stress and anxiety, which can interfere with falling asleep. Mindfulness practices encourage being present in the moment, allowing you to detach from racing thoughts and worries that might keep you awake at night. Incorporating these practices into your evening routine can signal to your body that it's time to wind down and prepare for sleep.

A good mindfulness practice involves deliberately focusing on the present moment without judgment. One common technique is mindful breathing, where you direct your attention to your breath as you inhale and exhale, noticing the sensation and rhythm of each breath. Another approach is body scan meditation, where you mentally explore and observe each part of your body, from head to toe, acknowledging any sensations without trying to change them. Guided mindfulness meditations, available through apps or recordings, can also be helpful, as they provide gentle prompts to keep your attention centered and guide you through the process.

The key to mindfulness is non-judgmental awareness – observing your thoughts, feelings, and sensations as they arise without attaching any value or criticism to them.

Additionally, gentle yoga or stretching can help release physical tension and promote relaxation, contributing to a more comfortable and restful sleep experience.

Inducing Natural Melatonin

Melatonin is a natural hormone the pineal gland produces in response to darkness. It is crucial in regulating your sleep-wake cycle, also known as your circadian rhythm. When it's dark, your body releases more melatonin, signaling it's time to wind down and prepare for sleep. Exposure to bright light, especially blue light from screens, can suppress melatonin production and disrupt your body's natural sleep signals.

While melatonin supplements can provide short-term relief, they may not address the underlying causes of sleep disruption and may lead to dependency over time.

Establish A Calming Sleep Routine

Wind down your day with activities like reading, gentle stretching, or sipping on a soothing herbal tea. Disconnect from the digital realm, letting go of the stimulating screen glow at least an hour before bed.

Craft A Sleep Sanctuary

Your bed should be reserved for sleep and relaxation. Keep it comfortable and serene, free from the distractions of work or entertainment. Creating a tranquil environment primes your brain for slumber.

Embrace Darkness

Exposure to artificial light, especially blue light emitted by electronic devices, can suppress melatonin production and disrupt this natural sleep-wake cycle. Creating a dark sleeping environment helps counteract this interference. When the room is dark, our bodies receive the signal that it's nighttime, enhancing their ability to initiate and maintain deep sleep. It's recommended to eliminate or block out light sources in the sleeping environment. This can involve using blackout curtains, turning off electronic devices, and covering LED lights or other artificial illumination sources.

Set A Regular Sleep Schedule

Allow your body's internal clock to synchronize with the rhythms of the universe. The ideal amount of sleep can vary based on age and individual needs. Generally, adults should aim for 7 to 9 hours of sleep per night to support optimal cognitive function, mood regulation, and overall health. For children, the recommended sleep duration varies based on age: preschoolers (3-5 years old) should aim for 10-13 hours, school-age children (6-13 years old) typically need 9-11 hours, and adolescents (14-17 years old) may benefit from 8-10 hours of sleep to promote proper growth and development.

Many of us find that our ADHD symptoms are rooted in a combination of multiple causes, in some cases, everything mentioned in this book, and more. My family discovered that all the things mentioned above contributed to our symptoms, so we made some major lifestyle and diet changes.

Because of that, I have provided a guide to chasing the ADHD zebra after this book and a brief chapter about embracing your uniqueness.
Before we get to that part, let's look at some other, less common, culprits to explore.

13
Get A Load Of This Shit

My research and experience have shown that each of the following health disturbances and environmental factors could mimic ADHD symptoms and may be worth exploring.

Inconsistent Environments

Imagine a home environment where the atmosphere shifts as quickly as the wind. Perhaps as a child, one day, you're applauded for your free-spirited creativity, and the next, you're standing in the corner for not following the rules to the letter. Discipline may be based on one parent's or the other's current mood.

On the other hand, picture this: you're an adult juggling work, relationships, and life's many demands. When life is smooth sailing, you're riding the wave of productivity, but when shit hits the fan, you struggle to stay on track.

This dance of conflicting situations can result in impulsiveness and inconsistencies in an individual's personality that mirror the hallmarks of ADHD symptoms.

Consider the scenario of someone constantly second-guessing their decisions, so they are switching from one task to the next, avoiding completion of any project. They are anxious that any mistake in the finished product will result in disappointment. This person's behavior may look like ADHD, but it could simply be the residue of growing up in an environment where perfection was the only standard worthy of praise.

Similarly, imagine another individual who's always acting impulsively to gain attention or a fleeting sense of validation. These actions might not purely be ADHD impulsivity but a response to an upbringing where love was conditional upon fleeting moments of success. This same attention-seeking behavior could also be a masking mechanism created to cover up a person's shortcomings.

How about in a home where bedtime is 8 pm one night and 10 pm the next, or fighting with a sibling is punishable one day, but the next, the parent is exhausted, and they let it slide? These inconsistencies can cause chaos inside one's mind. Never having consistent standards, the mind becomes a wild free-for-all mimicking ADHD.

The fact is, our immediate family, environment, and social circle are all things that can shape our behavior and reactions. Imagine a circle of friends who constantly undermine your goals or a partner who consistently dismisses your aspirations. These assholes can magnify your doubts, causing inconsistencies in behavior and racing thoughts.

The solution: Surround yourself with supportive people. If you are a parent, do your best to create a consistent environment. Even with hard boundary setting and clear communication, these dynamics won't dissolve overnight. They require consistent effort, ongoing conversations, and the courage to redefine your family and social dynamics in favor of emotional well-being.

Learned ADHD Behaviors

Who doesn't want to be the first to dig into a yummy meal? Who wouldn't love to score the first spot in a long line? Does anyone WANT to clean their room or house?

As a child, we're taught the importance of patience. We're taught not to skip lines because it's rude. We're taught to clean up our toys when we're done playing. And for some, even better than being taught, they are led by example: Mom lets everyone make their plate first. Dad directs the family to the back of the line, where they wait patiently. Mom and Dad work together, picking up the house at the end of the night to start fresh the next day.

These dynamics we witness can become our habits and behaviors.

I remember my mom insisting that the dishes were done, and the sink cleaned before bed. I remember her saying, "No one likes to wake up to a sink full of dishes."

Now, for some reason, as an adult, on some crazy subconscious level, I cannot stand waking up to a sink full of dishes!

So what happens in a household where mom screams when frustrated and dad is incredibly impatient? What happens when everything is so chaotic that no tasks are ever completed? A child in that environment is likely to respond by mimicking this behavior.

Moreso, Imagine a living environment that is an unorganized disaster.

These things imprint on us and become part of how we react, how our mind works, and how we care for our environment. This is what I call "Learned ADHD."

Sensory Disorders and Their Impact on Cognitive Function

Sensory processing challenges can indeed mimic ADHD symptoms, leading to difficulties in attention, focus, and behavior regulation. Individuals with sensory disorders may struggle with sensory integration, making it hard to filter and process sensory stimuli. This inability to process stimuli can manifest as restlessness, impulsivity, and difficulty concentrating, all ADHD traits. Addressing sensory sensitivities involves creating sensory-friendly environments, incorporating sensory tools, and seeking sensory integration therapy.

Mood Disorders and Their Connection to ADHD-Like Symptoms

The intricate relationship between mood disorders and cognitive function often leads to overlapping symptoms with ADHD. Anxiety, depression, and bipolar disorder can all share traits with ADHD, such as inattention, irritability, and emotional dysregulation. It's essential to recognize that mood disorders can exacerbate or even mimic ADHD symptoms. Integrating holistic approaches like therapy, mindfulness, and mood-regulating nutrition can aid in managing both mood disorders and ADHD-like symptoms.

Thyroid Dysfunction and Hormone Imbalances

Thyroid health and hormonal balance are crucial in cognitive function. Thyroid dysfunction, especially hypo- or hyperthyroidism, can lead to difficulties in concentration, memory, and mood regulation. Hormonal imbalances, including fluctuations in cortisol and sex hormones, can also impact cognitive performance and behavior. Addressing hormone-related challenges involves seeking medical assessment, optimizing thyroid health, and adopting holistic approaches like stress management, sleep, and proper nutrition.

Vision and Hearing Problems

Visual and auditory challenges can contribute to attention and focus difficulties. Visual impairments, such as uncorrected refractive errors, can strain cognitive resources as individuals struggle to process visual information.

Similarly, hearing problems can lead to misunderstandings, difficulty following instructions, and reduced attention. Regular vision and hearing assessments are essential to ensure optimal sensory function.

Seizures and Tourette Syndrome

Seizure disorders and Tourette syndrome can share symptoms with ADHD, creating diagnostic challenges. Seizures can lead to inattention, memory lapses, and cognitive fluctuations.

Similarly, Tourette syndrome, characterized by involuntary movements and vocalizations, can lead to distractibility and impulsivity. Acknowledging the potential overlap and seeking medical evaluation is vital to distinguishing these conditions from ADHD.

Neural Proteins & Neurotransmitters

Neurotransmitters are chemicals that transmit signals between neurons in the brain. Dopamine plays a crucial role in various brain functions, including regulating mood, motivation, reward, and movement.

Neural proteins, on the other hand, are a diverse group of proteins involved in the structure, function, and communication of neurons. These proteins perform various roles, from maintaining neuron health to facilitating neurotransmitter release and supporting synaptic connections.

Disruptions in neural proteins such as can impact neurotransmitter regulation, contributing to cognitive difficulties. Holistic support for neural proteins includes nutrition, hydration, adequate sleep, physical activity, mental stimulation, social engagement, and mindfulness.

Up Next: A System Built For Compliance

Now let's take someone with some or all of these: a sensitive mind, exposure to toxins, vitamin deficiencies, food intolerance, gene mutations, gut disturbances, and maybe even a not-so-great home life, and throw them into the fiery pits of the most chaotic environment that exists today: the public school. We'll now explore how a broken system can add salt to the deep wounds of someone with a neurodivergent mind and ADHD symptoms.

14
Day Don't Care

The **system** is broken, not you.

In the movie "Divergent," based on the popular book series by Veronica Roth, society is divided into five different factions based on dominant personality traits. Each "faction" represents a distinct category of people: Abnegation (selflessness), Amity (peacefulness), Candor (honesty), Dauntless (bravery), and Erudite (intellect).

The protagonist, Tris, discovers that not only does she not fit neatly into any single category, she can excel at all of them, making her "Divergent" and a threat to the established order.

While our reality may not be the world depicted in "Divergent," our diversity is very similar. We all have unique strengths, weaknesses, and problem-solving styles that contribute to the makeup of humanity. The issue is that our education system is ideal for $\frac{1}{6}$ of the population; it's a daycare built to create a compliant workforce, and if you can't fit into the box - you're left to fend for yourself.

When neurodivergent kids like Tris in the movie threaten the established one-size-fits-all order of things, they are often labeled disobedient.

Once a child is labeled as "bad" in the system, they become the target of every single mishap. Fifty-six kids could all break the same rule, but the child with the label will take the brunt of the punishment and ridicule. If a neurodivergent child causes chaos in a classroom, it is instantly the child's fault, and blame is never placed on the actual structure, dynamics, and environment of the classroom or the teacher. Why? Because the public school framework assumes that all students will thrive in a standardized environment, following the same curriculum, learning at the same pace, and adhering to the same expectations. Therefore, if something goes wrong, it must be the fault of the "bad apple" rather than the system itself, right?

Just before COVID closed the schools (6th grade for my boys), I received a call from a teacher claiming that my child was clowning around in math class. I took a good look in the mirror, reflecting on my childhood behaviors, and told the teacher that many kids who clown or joke are masking that they don't understand the lesson. They would rather look funny to their peers than look inferior. So I then asked, "Is my child understanding the curriculum?" Instantly dismissing my theory, her reply, "he understands just fine. He is just looking for attention."

When the schools closed that March, and I had my kids at home, I could grasp exactly what they understood so far in a safe and understanding environment. Not to my surprise, my kids were showing an understanding of math at a 4th-grade level. Which says to me that somewhere in 5th grade, they fell behind. Of course, this was the year of the psychopath teacher, the unruly principal, anxiety attack, and the reaction to medications - it all made sense, and proved my theory of "clowning" to be correct.

We continued homeschooling long after the schools opened back up, and within two years, my kids went from understanding 4th-grade math to dominating algebra ahead of their peers! I'm not making claims that homeschooling is superior or that I am a fabulous teacher, more so stating that with a new environment mixed with a bit of love and understanding - any kid can thrive - even those labeled as "bad."

They needed someone to look past the behavioral mask and discover they were lost, but they didn't and my boys were left to fend for themselves. I believe there was a point where they finally said, "Screw it, you think I'm bad? Then I'm going to be just that." We had to walk away from that environment and start new.

Some extraordinary humans teach in the public school system but are limited in time and have ridiculous expectations passed down from federal and state governments.

The public school system's emphasis on standardized testing as the primary measure of success places pressure on students and teachers!

Here are some things to look for if your child struggles in school

Comprehension: Do they understand? ADHD is not a low IQ disorder. The inability to focus is not a sign of a lack of intelligence. Have the child removed from the classroom and test their understanding in a different environment. If they have the comprehension, move on to the following few questions.

Surroundings: Are they distracted because the classroom environment is unruly? In 5th grade, my son's classroom was full of children running around, throwing things at each other, yelling, and a teacher (literally) banging her head off the wall. I had to get permission from the principal to allow him to wear a hooded sweatshirt or a beanie hat during class to drown out the chaos around him. I made several unacknowledged complaints to the school about the classroom environment. My biggest regret was not knowing my voice then and not understanding how to advocate for my child. If your child is learning in a chaotic environment, it is your right to move that child to a different classroom or school. Get to know your rights and your options. Never think that you are out of line when advocating for your child. You do not want to have the same regrets as me.

Social: The social aspect of school can often be a significant source of distraction for students. The dynamics of friendships, peer pressure, and even bullying can consume a student's thoughts and emotional well-being, hindering their ability to engage in the academic aspect of school fully. When children are preoccupied with social situations, whether it's a conflict with friends, a desire for acceptance, or the fear of being made fun of, their attention and energy may be diverted away from their studies. I recommend a check-in to make sure this isn't causing existing symptoms to worsen.

Lack of interest: ADHD symptoms or not, I find it hard to believe anyone can read a book cover to cover if the story sucks. Sometimes, these kids are simply bored and disinterested, and quite frankly, kids and teens shouldn't be sitting still for 8 hours per day. Anyway, it's quite unnatural!

Most phone calls I received from the school were about compliance. They were up out of their chairs, talking when not supposed to, and pushing back against authority. I never once received a call with concerns or praise about academics - ya know, the main damn reason they are there for 8 hours.

The school's main focus lies in district test scores and behavior modification.

As a parent, I don't want to raise children who are completely submissive and scared to speak their minds. I'll just be over here teaching them respectful ways to challenge authority and let their unique minds change this world.

Don't let a broken system be the main reason you think something is wrong with you.. Simply put, if you are experiencing anything mentioned, it's no secret that you have a unique mind, perhaps a sensitive mind. You were made to change the world. You just need to get those pesky negative symptoms under control first.

15

You Are A Neurodivergent Badass!

In a world that often seeks conformity, embracing neurodiversity is like embracing the vibrant colors of a kaleidoscope.

Neurodivergent individuals, or as I referred to earlier, those with a sensitive mind, possess various amazing qualities, bringing fresh perspectives, creativity, and unique problem-solving skills to the table of humanity.

This divergence isn't a deficit; it's a blessing that is pretty freaking fantastic, especially once your adverse reactions to the environment, food, and toxic substances are managed.

Consider the way you or someone you know with "ADHD" can immerse themselves in hyperfocus, diving into a subject with an intensity that few can match. Think of the empathetic lens through which an individual with autism views the world. Neurodivergent minds often shine in art, technology, science, and innovation, offering insights and breakthroughs that propel humanity forward.

Throughout history, remarkable individuals have broken out of the system's box of norms and embraced their unique identities. Visionaries like Albert Einstein, who revolutionized physics, and Temple Grandin, who revolutionized the understanding of autism, have shown us that these glitches in the mind are a sign of genius.

While you're focusing on chasing zebras to eliminate the challenges your negative symptoms cause you to face, I also encourage you to embrace the strengths that accompany your unique mind.

Let's Chase Zebras, Not Squirrels.

I have combined my experience, research, and education to develop this "ADHD Zebra Chasing Guide." Use this guide alongside your trusted healthcare professional if you feel there could be more to your story. You want to get to the root of your symptoms rather than spend the rest of your life masking them.

1. Refer to Chapter 3 and do a thorough environment check. Are your relationships consistent with your values? Is your parenting consistent with that of your spouse? When your children are not in your care, are they in a calm environment?
2. Install a reverse osmosis or high-quality water filtration system in your home to avoid dangerous chemicals lurking in public water systems.
3. Establish a sleep schedule. Create a relaxing environment. Stay consistent.
4. Seek help from a natural doctor, such as a chiropractor or physical therapist, to check for retained primitive reflexes. Follow up by doing exercises to eliminate any that you have retained. Remember that this may not be the end-all-be-all fix to your ADHD symptoms, but it is a great start. Also, inquire with a professional about stimulating the vagus nerve to assist your gut-brain connection.
5. Order the following three tests with your trusted health professional to shed light on what is happening inside

your body: Organic Acids Test, MTHFR Genetic Test, Heavy Metal and Trace Elements Test.

6. Try an elimination diet. You may have to try several times to make things easier and explore several trigger foods. The most common culprits are dairy, soy, wheat, corn, refined sugar, artificial dyes, sugars, and preservatives.

7. Seek therapy for chronic stress and trauma. Cognitive Behavioral Therapy is important even after minimizing your symptoms, as behaviors can become hard-to-break habits over the years.

8. Remove yourself or your child from inconsistent environments and seek help from a therapist to rebuild your family and mental mindscape.

Remember, there is no quick-fix pill to good physical, spiritual, or mental health; progress doesn't happen overnight.

You are not broken; you are maybe just bent - but either way, you are a badass and will change the world. Good Luck.

About The Author

Jessica Carrier is a dynamic force in the world of holistic health, nutrition, and neurodiversity advocacy. She is the accomplished author of "Eat Clean 21" A 21-Day Nutritional Cleanse for Releasing Heavy Metals and toxins, with a comprehensive guide that empowers individuals to transform their health, nourish their bodies, enhance brain function, and reset their metabolism through clean eating.

Jessica's journey into holistic health and nutrition was deeply influenced by her own experiences with ADHD. Her dedication to understanding and managing her and her children's condition led her to become a Holistic Health Practitioner (HHP) and a Certified Transformational Nutrition Coach (CTNC).

As a mother of twin boys and veteran of the United States Air Force, Jessica brings a unique perspective to her work. She is a multifaceted entrepreneur who has built multiple successful businesses and harnessed her passion for photography, coffee, and nutrition to create a unique blend of holistic wellness and creative entrepreneurship.

Jessica is not only a fervent advocate for children who are diagnosed with ADHD, but also a strong supporter of mental health awareness.

Her unyielding commitment to challenging the status quo is evident in her decision to homeschool her own children.

Jessica inspires positive change in the lives of many, fostering a greater understanding of neurodiversity and holistic well-being. Her advocacy and dedication to healthier living resonate throughout her work, making her a prominent figure in the field of holistic brain health.

For Jessica, nutrition encompasses more than just food. Her focus is uncovering the root cause of dis-ease and treating the whole person physically, mentally, and spiritually.

I didn't just make this shit up!

1. Goyette P, Sumner JS, Milos R, Duncan AM, Rosenblatt DS, Matthews RG, Rozen R. Human methylenetetrahydrofolate reductase: isolation of cDNA, mapping and mutation identification. Nat Genet. 1994 Jun;7(2):195-200. doi: 10.1038/ng0694-195. Erratum in: Nat Genet. 1994 Aug;7(4):551. PMID: 7920641.

2. Parsley Health. (2018). MTHFR Mutation: How it Affects Your Health and What to Do. Parsley Health Blog. https://www.parsleyhealth.com/blog/mthfr-mutation/

3. Jafari T, Rostampour N, Fallah AA, Hesami A. The association between mercury levels and autism spectrum disorders: A systematic review and meta-analysis. J Trace Elem Med Biol. 2017 Dec;44:289-297. doi: 10.1016/j.jtemb.2017.09.002. Epub 2017 Sep 4. PMID: 28965590.

4. CDC's Agency for Toxic Substances and Disease Registry. (n.d.). Who is at Risk of Lead Exposure? Retrieved from https://www.atsdr.cdc.gov/csem/leadtoxicity/who_at_risk.html

5. Braun, J. M., Hornung, R., Chen, A., Dietrich, K. N., Jacobs, D. E., Jones, R., ... & Lanphear, B. P. (2017). Effect of Residential Lead-Exposure on Blood Pressure in Children. JAMA Pediatrics, 171(3), 274-281. doi:10.1001/jamapediatrics.2016.4136

6. Jusko, T. A., Henderson, C. R., Lanphear, B. P., Cory-Slechta, D. A., Parsons, P. J., Canfield, R. L., ... & Bellinger, D. C. (2017). Blood lead concentrations < 10 μg/dL and child intelligence at 6 years of age. Environmental Health Perspectives, 125(6), 670-676. https://www.ncbi.nlm.nih.gov/pmc/articles/PMC5289032/

7. Lanphear, B. P., Hornung, R., Khoury, J., Yolton, K., Baghurst, P., Bellinger, D. C., ... & Braun, J. (2005). Low-level environmental lead exposure and children's intellectual function: an international pooled analysis. PLoS medicine, 3(4), e99. doi:10.1371/journal.pmed.0030099

8. Boucher O, Jacobson SW, Plusquellec P, Dewailly E, Ayotte P, Forget-Dubois N, Jacobson JL, Muckle G. Prenatal methylmercury, postnatal lead exposure, and evidence of attention-deficit/hyperactivity disorder among Inuit children in Arctic Québec. Environ Health Perspect. 2012 Oct;120(10):1456-61. doi: 10.1289/ehp.1204976. Epub 2012 Sep 21. PMID: 23008274; PMCID: PMC3491943.

9. Jafari T, Rostampour N, Fallah AA, Hesami A. The association between mercury levels and autism spectrum disorders: A systematic review and

meta-analysis. J Trace Elem Med Biol. 2017 Dec;44:289-297. doi: 10.1016/j.jtemb.2017.09.002. Epub 2017 Sep 4. PMID: 28965590.

10. Klotz K, Weistenhöfer W, Neff F, Hartwig A, van Thriel C, Drexler H. The Health Effects of Aluminum Exposure. Dtsch Arztebl Int. 2017 Sep 29;114(39):653-659. doi: 10.3238/arztebl.2017.0653. PMID: 29034866; PMCID: PMC5651828.

11. Rodríguez-Barranco, M., Lacasaña, M., Aguilar-Garduño, C., Alguacil, J., Gil, F., González-Alzaga, B., & Rojas-García, A. (2013). Association of arsenic, cadmium and manganese exposure with neurodevelopment and behavioral disorders in children: A systematic review and meta-analysis. Science of The Total Environment, Volumes 454–455, Pages 562-577. ISSN 0048-9697. https://doi.org/10.1016/j.scitotenv.2013.03.047.

12. National Toxicology Program, Draft NTP Monograph on the Systematic Review of Fluoride Exposure and Neurodevelopmental and Cognitive Health Effects. 2020. [(accessed on 31 March 2023)]. Available online: https://fluoridealert.org/wp-content/uploads/ntp.revised-monograph.9-16-2020.pdf [PubMed]

13. Fiore G, Veneri F, Di Lorenzo R, Generali L, Vinceti M, Filippini T. Fluoride Exposure and ADHD: A Systematic Review of Epidemiological Studies. Medicina (Kaunas). 2023 Apr 19;59(4):797. doi: 10.3390/medicina59040797. PMID: 37109754; PMCID: PMC10143272.

14. Dr. Rebecca Bevans, a true authority with a Master's degree in Child Development and a Ph.D. in Cognitive Neuroscience, has made a significant mark by highlighting the alarming risks associated with artificial food colors. Search "The Effects of Artificial Food Dyes - Dr. Rebecca Bevans."

15. Arnold LE, Lofthouse N, Hurt E. Artificial food colors and attention-deficit/hyperactivity symptoms: conclusions to dye for. Neurotherapeutics. 2012 Jul;9(3):599-609. doi: 10.1007/s13311-012-0133-x. PMID: 22864801; PMCID: PMC3441937.

16. Miller, M. D., Steinmaus, C., Golub, M. S., Castorina, R., Thilakarathne, R., Bradman, A., & Marty, M. A. (2022). Potential impacts of synthetic food dyes on activity and attention in children: a review of the human and animal evidence. Environmental Health, 21(1), 45. https://doi.org/10.1186/s12940-022-00806-8

17. Pelsser LM, Frankena K, Toorman J, Savelkoul HF, Pereira RR, Buitelaar JK. A randomized controlled trial into the effects of food on ADHD. Eur Child Adolesc Psychiatry. 2009 Jan;18(1):12-9. doi: 10.1007/s00787-008-0695-7. Epub 2008 Apr 21. PMID: 18431534.

Printed in the USA
CPSIA information can be obtained
at www.ICGtesting.com
LVHW012308020424
776257LV00006B/301